sandmaps is the property
of RLFPA Editions (OPC) Pvt Ltd — an imprint of RædLeaf Foundation
for Poetry & Allied Arts (since 2012), not-for-profit, an independent
literary organization committed to promoting poetry and allied arts in
India and abroad.

This book is a work of fiction. Any references to historical events, real people, or real places are fictional. Other names, characters, places, and events are products of the author's imagination and any resemblance to actual events or places, living or dead, is entirely coincidental.

Copyright © 2020 by Vasuki Subbarao

No part of this book may be reproduced or transmitted in any form or by any means, electronic, mechanical, photocopying, or otherwise, without the express written consent of RLFPA Editions (OPC) Pvt Ltd.

For more information about permission to reuse any material from this book, please contact rlfpaeditions.biz@gmail.com. Visit rlpoetry.org for more. Contact +91 9326776610

First Publication Date: September 2020
ISBN: 978-81-939295-9-9
₹300 | US $12.99
Originally Published in Paperback
Cover Design: Linda Ashok

Manufactured in India, published & funded
by RLFPA Editions (OPC) Pvt Ltd.

sandmaps

Poems by vasuki subbarao

INTRODUCTION

The last few days of every trip here—
I see my mind detach itself
from the body which has been derailed
by strangling crowds, fumes,
and streams of sweat flowing
down its dried-up river banks—

To go on a shopping spree,
stuffing my pockets with India,
shirt-pockets with the North
of Vindhyas and trousers with the South,
buying the country with a flash
of my American Express card, no cash.

I'll have two Kashmirs, please.
Do you accept credit cards?
You don't need to gift wrap them,
it'll take space.
I'll have a few begging bowls
(they come for free sir),
a few smiling faces
(they come without teeth sir),

a line of colourful vessels in front of a public tap.

(you have to take this as carry-on sir),
hugs and tears
(I'll carry them in my heart please),
and memories, lots and lots of them
(sir, sir, you forgot to take all of them),

that pass through a labyrinth
of security checks and scanners,
(they cannot find any metal inside, only sand),
standing incongruous in front
of a derisive immigration official at NY airport.
"Empty all your pockets please," he scorns,
"and your heart too."

He sifts India around, which lies
on his tabletop in bits and pieces
like a jigsaw puzzle that has befuddled history,

emptying my shoes next to pour
out sand grains into a map
of faces and trysts that charm
him with a candour that could turn
body scan beeps into sweet jingles.

He lets the entire map through
on the fast lane and sends me
packing to detention for human
trafficking,

waiting, and waiting,

with only half an India in my pockets,
and a fully laden heart.

When I start preparing for one of my trips to India or any other country for that matter, I am not ashamed to admit that I am a typical over prepared plebian tourist. I start with a fast run to the local library and come back home with a stack load of travel guides, those neatly packed parcels of places and spells, elaborate gifts of space and time. These books promise to deliver places and events directly to my doorsteps without budging an inch.

This is the age when even the Marco Polos and Vikings have been reduced to a family of four in a luxury sedan. My preparedness leaves me with nothing to be explored but only to be seen; no unknown to be conquered, only the known to be confirmed. My knowledge precedes and supersedes my imagination. The information I gather is such a tough act to follow that places seem pale in comparison to the colours that precede them like the diminutive and middling profile of a matinee idol hiding behind his billboard.

And then it is time for this killjoy to leave home finally. Travel books have been returned to the library to avoid late fees, and only a cheap map makes it to my suitcase as a disaster recovery plan for a smartphone gone out of charge. This map slowly makes its way from my suitcase to my rucksack to my hand and finally into my pockets, crumpling though every transition to a point where the original lines blend and blur with my crumples.

Somewhere halfway through the trip, I misplace the 10th and last copy of the itinerary that I had strategically located in all my travel paraphernalia before I left home. And my world comes apart thrown to the wolves of happenstance.

The original lines in the map have by now totally given way to the crumples. And that is when my trip goes out of the script, and every crumple leads to a serendipitous dead-end.

The smile of a schoolgirl perched on her dad's scooter as I whiz past them in an auto-rickshaw. The man who puts Google to shame by walking me safe for 2 miles to an unknown address. The old lady who walks on her hands up the 9000 steps of Adam's Peak in Sri Lanka reaching the peak at 5 AM just in time for the sunrise. And the farmer who asks me to make an entry in his passbook as I stand in line at the bank cash counter right below scores of entries, each made by a stranger I have never met but feel connected to through this cosmic ledger.

Slowly but surely I am no longer scared of entropy, that suburbanite's nemesis. This is when I also start looking for history, not in its ruins but the fresh grass weeds growing all around them like a cordon of parodies. Not in its glorified battles, but in the sandwiched struggles of culture to stay alive. I start looking for a circle on its tangents. I find great things to buy in the free advertisements displayed behind the billboards. I go looking for a hideout of ants under a colossal boulder seeking comfort under a millstone.

I, who spend most of my time sorting out dots to arrange them in a pattern that best suits me, connect them in an attempt to reveal an aggregate; an all-encompassing truth. I finally come to terms with them and they with me. And when things are starting to go right (or totally wrong depending on your perspective), I find that 10th copy of my itinerary inside the hotel dustbin. The plan is back on track after a few dustings and sanitary sprays. There are places to be seen and ticked, photos to be taken with family plonked in front of all monuments (or should I say monuments plonked behind family), unmissable events and sunsets, and India (or any 3rd world country) to be bought at a discount, appointments to be kept and a smattering of final goodbyes to be bid.

Now it is finally time to go back home and shove entropy under the doormat (what was I thinking). As we sink into our plane seats and dab our dust-ridden cheeks with a wet towel, all serendipitous experiences are relegated to the sand grains that I cannot seem to shake off from my worn-out shoes (time to get a new pair of shoes again I tell myself).

Withstanding resounding thuds on doormats across continents and snuggling under the crevices in my shoes like poor migrants huddling over one another at the dark corner of a beaten-up truck, these sand grains have the last laugh on me doing that song and dance show in front of the immigration official sending me to detention, leaving me a book of poems to write, one grain at a time, as I wait to be released by the gods at immigration.

Vasuki Subbarao
United States, 2020

CONTENTS

To Divya, for all hopes renewed.

sandmaps

Poems by **vasuki subbarao**

At a Movie Theatre, Bangalore: Surreal Economics

Two kids in a row
for the balcony and the front seats,
awaiting entry into a dreamland;
me, a bed tucked in my arms,
and he, a mat.

Dialogues leak through
as greetings that welcome
— the stars are here
to meet them.

The windows open
to the shafts of sunlight
Their dreams split ways
for the double matinee
to beam.

One of them with cheeks
pressed against the gates,
begs for a view —
a silent protest against
the flag that promised one to all.

Maybe it is inversely proportional;
a dream to the cost of its fulfilment?
But surely, the gate is the threshold!

At Parthasarathy Temple, Madras: Close Encounters

a priest, alone
beside him, a nervous flame;
shadow soaked in oil.

i

the devotees
clean up after themselves
faith. broken nuts. blessings.

ii

In his yawns,
they hear mantras
in the slits of his doubt, rituals…

i

the Gods receive
a peel-no-bleed; a baring
of craft; organs that sink

ii

the slow threat
of a nebula prepares
him for the next dawn.

a priest, alone
beside him, a nervous flame;
shadow soaked in oil.

Visiting a Relative, Bangalore: Rude Signs

In a house with a granny,
and a mosquito trapped in a net.

[only one scheming an escape]

Her senses sway
to the sounds of *suprabhatam*
The mosquito,
 beyond her covenant;
        a distant temple in ruins.

When the smog ports
for her to load some pills
the mosquito girdles her being

The smell of *agarbatti*
from the room of Gods,
spreads like a proud corpse.

Soon, granny will be
on the knees of gravity for a return
Until then, the mosquito & she

        mode: repeat

At Painted Desert, Arizona: Tumbleweed Home

A patch of earth floats
in his mind,
dust in his soles;
roots are arrows shot
from the banyan sky.

How can a native ask for a land?
How can his hands that dot
the map astral the paper?
How can eyes be embedded
in sight; how can their feet rest
that never tread an inch?

A genealogical festoon
a land is not a geyser.
Clay cannot sculpt itself
So, you may call it a body's leash
on a wandering mind,
womb housing a tumbleweed.

At Home, Washington D.C.: My Wife on the Sofa

what is in front of me?

a caricature
hogged out of dead air?

a cut-out of life
propping the ether?

a cave holding
a rock in place?

an invisible hand
that draws a body around breath?

a hurler of shadows,
a geyser of ideas,
a bivouac for *Vayu's* army?

a medium fancying itself to be a node,
a mirror in front of an image,
senses trapped in a cage
a voice signal of distress

what is this silhouette
that rocks the hazy edge
of melancholia?

**Revisiting the Hospital where my Father Died, Princeton,
U.S.A.: Late Beginnings**

Anna,
it has not been easy
keeping you alive ever
since you made me click
that switch in the morgue.

Wails and sweet words were easy.
And so were tunnels of distant
looks, innocent smiles and
obituaries in fine print.

But then it got harder,
and the pressure mounted,
as your memories got slowly
dislodged in a clamour for bites
by memories more progressive;

as your memories went second-
hand relying on cheap props,
prompts and staged events.

And slowly but surely,
like the last syllable of a
dying language that is slipping
out of that Andean woman's tongue
into an abyss of lost words,
your grace is hanging onto
the edge of my failing floppies.

Anna, your death has only just begun.
And it is a long way home.

To a Friend with Twins, Princeton: Lifetime Guarantee

I have to give it to you, Oh God.
Five millenniums of the human sleuth

going after your secrets,
ransacking every clue
or decoy you have laid in his path,
to stare at an answer bare
till it clothed itself back with a mark;

and yet you have stayed ahead,
as your pants guide his ears.

Five millenniums of abuse,
of clogging and fraying the mesh,
and yet your filters sieve fine as ever,
as soot and metalwork in sync
to wake me up from a nightmare

where fruits were filled with mud,
clouds rained dirt of body and soul,
cemetery flowers wilted on bloom,

and wrinkles lined a newborn's visage,
as viruses of *samskara* pervaded
its cells and lust sunk into its pupils;

into a bright new dawn not stained
by the hues of yesterday, as goods smuggled
in through the night were seized
at the shores and sent back.

I have to give it to you, Oh God.
At least for now!

At Anand Bhavan, Allahabad: Tautology

From his cradle under the sky,
man cups the globe in his palms,
tucking the map in his pocket

From his vexing systolic,
he sweeps the human canvas
From his toilet seat, he leaps
into the thrones of power

His fingertip burnt by
the nerves of mortality;
from his bowl of fears,
sprouts a fist, determined

His watch wraps around the wrists
of time, his room is a stage
where his voice wicks
its way through a drum of wax

This is only the micro
The macro sits in our fancies

    When the expanse
is a glutton of space;
    no eternity but a click;

When there's no paddy field
      beyond a rice grain.

At Nanjangud Train Station, Karnataka: Crystal Bowl

Under the shade of a *Peepal* tree,
they weave baskets & chairs—

      —for the tree to
gather its leaves & rest its bark

As the knife carves long strips
from a log, the tree winces
in pain like a mother standing next
to her kid at a clinic
Feeling its bark in reflex
the shade quivers in fear

Mind if I call the
baskets and chairs the crystal bowls
presenting a dimming future?

The wicket fans
sees the death of its breeze,
The wooden strips carve
a slit in its shade

As a massive wind passes by

& a leaf falls into a finished basket,
waiting for the lid in the weave.

On Railway Platform, Bangalore Station: Best Silver

a travelling hall of mirrors,

in which my dignity reflects
on a kid defecating on the sidewalk

in which my hopes rebound
from the ruins as dust into my eyes

in which my vigour trapped
in the yawn of a derelict
before it knocks my knees.

in which my longevity
leaps off the ashes, & my health
squirts from a leper's sores

It is a *maya*
where I try to break free
from the conjugated sum
of cracked numerals

All I am left hoping for,
shamed by the mirrors around me,
is to be a good mirror to someone,
and be their feast;

Not to like what I see in the glass,
but just be the best silver around.

At Holocaust Memorial, Washington D.C.: My Amigo

You knocked on my
door late at night,
inviting yourself onto my couch
like an old friend.

      You were tired but not beat.
      There was no blood dripping from your gums.
      Your face was not knotted by dread.

You were happy about
a mission accomplished,
proud of a job well done,
for having tried to balance his sheets.

But you were concerned
That this was slipping away from you.

That pogrom had given way to
skirmishes, cataclysms had stooped
down to page 9 stories and shades
of grey had eaten up the
edges to rule the roost over the whole
scale, confounding you into inaction.

There will always be tomorrow
you said as you sipped your bourbon,

      to douse it down.

At Talakaveri, Karnataka: Self-Doubt

Wires run
on tall poles along
a small mountain stream

hauling electricity
for temples & huts
as river-current, below,
is future on a backtrack

I carry a small lamp
to *Kaveri** & say,

*"Look at all this energy
you will weave downstream,
how much power you'll assume,
what eminence you'll wear,
& the lives you'll illume?"*

Kaveri, shy, trickles away
in disbelief; *"happy
to be a stream carefree*

*not ready to embrace my future,
to fathom my depth."*

** Source of River Kavery in the Western Ghats*

Along a Village Road in Karnataka: Scale 1000:1

How much land
does a mountain occupy?
How much dirt
makes a pile?

In an ocean of paddy,
a tremulous hamlet
watches over

waves of crop
swept ashore
to the foothills
of hungry skyscrapers;

As rivers risk their lives
plunging a million feet
to die the death of a flash

How much earth
needs a man, I muse,
as the third dimension enslaves
the other in a map wrinkled out-of-scale.

At the Giza Pyramids, Egypt: Vandalized Courtrooms

All the cold math that went in here
is talking back to me now,
bruised equations begging
me to free them from the blind
faith that enchained them.

All the servile body frames
plead with me to remove the
arc of the tangent drawn plumb
along their hunched backs by pen
holders that masqueraded as scribes.

All these ladders built to reach
the sky attic point me down
the cellar stairs to the earth's womb
at the end of a stepped umbilical
where awaiting me is a kingdom
of mummies, man-made fossils in a
gift wrap.

I call the court into session again,
decreeing that death had been just
an interlude and reign justice
as vandals lurk in the shadows.

At the Barber Shop, Mysore: Close Shave

the touch:
nothing sexual about it

not the serpentine clasp
of two bodies headed for coitus,
but rather a fortuitous graze

scissors that clip your nerves
a stethoscope that traces your pulse
ageing palms that calm your blood
and her youth that sculpts your breath

as social rules sizzle
the spine of a man a loner.
a vagrant wind moves the caged heart
a ball of flame steadily withdraws

it's like a stranger's eye raking up
the natives from their hearths,
like a monsoon's first shower
easing in with a sublime joy

the touch;
how it pleasantly numbs my frame
as the barber nears my ears.

At Roadside Bus Stop, Near Bangalore: Molehills

Is this an old man's face
by the road, or a montage of history,
a sanctuary of events,
an asylum of dates…

The face is the last resort
where wheels screech to a halt,
and lines mark their tread;

where floods trickle in streams,
hills shrink into moles,
forests autumn his scalp,
and oceans shore on his lap

Borders of nature and man,
sink into his skin; he spittles
paan; a blotch of riot

His *beedi* curls up
the smoke from every gun,
as destiny shrugs on his man

So much for his face;
It is in his hands
the fate of my next poem.

Walking in an Alley, Bangalore: Sour Grapes

the doors are breasts,
to the prying sun

unabashed, its eyes
on a goose-chase run
along the dim-lit corridors

through the chorus
of sarees and anklets
out into the backyard

where the *tulsi*
contemplates proximity
of dust and distance

I ask the sun to fill me in
the long drawn intimacy
of the corridors

but it is dusk to render me full;
the sun has rushed down the corridor
out through the backyard into oblivion

…almost a muse and a sore neck.

Under a Tamarind Tree, Bangalore: Prison Concert

Trapped in a green tamarind
is my unborn child awaiting a fall?

Trapped in a blind girl's mind,
is an unmet image of the creator

In a sleepless eye is a dream
that will never cross the rivers of night.

 In a rock is the muted sound of history
 In a milestone is the journey of a man
 In a word is the meaning of silence
 In a monkey's tail is the stem of evolution
 In a beggar's specs is the clearing of a jungle
 In a marble is a child malformed in butterfly's wings.

Trapped in the shades of the past
is the story of the dead soldiers—
one heaped upon another

And God conducts this symphony
of pieces unseen and untold,
of life's last little secrets, and dear,

from behind the locked door of his shrine.

Near Parents' Home, Bangalore: Naming a Poem

Every morning,
a shepherd girl is busy
rounding up her letters for me—

her entire flock of twenty-six
she knows by name

"These are the vowels, my Lord.
Rest of the flock, purposeless,
depends on them."

      Is it the way my poetry
      feeds on her destitution?

"One of the vowels, my Lord, is missing;
 got stuck in some rut, so let's do without it.

"You go and beat up some dust &
by dusk on your return, I'll group my flock
into words; hitch the iambs to your meter.

Soon, there be a poem, headless,
& squish your night picked early."

Into the fields she goes with my poem,
leaving me to look for a title
in a sea of words.

Wading through the Crowds, Bombay: Hit Commercial

This land of poets where Gods
fetched rivers from a jug of water,
the sky from a patch of blue,
and the earth from a fist of mud,

      is now left with just the seeds.

This land of seers who drew
a circle of births and rebirths
around the nave of sufferance,

      is now a swarm of bodies falling weeds,
      in search of souls to match.

This land of souls who passed
through the earth on their way to *moksha*,
who spurned this turn for the next,

      now holds them back at a ransom,
      making every breathing skin a surfeit,
      and compost out of every death.

This land of savants who first grasped
the inequities of nature,

      is now a paragon that puts <u>it</u> to shame.

This is an ad that sold its canvas,
a sky that promised all the shelter,
a soil that vowed to be a foundation too,
rivers that offered all the tears,

a Samaritan who had given so much,
that his hands dropped off by wear,

      right into the cupped arms of a child.

Driving through a Sleeping Town, Madras Road:
Navratri Year Around

The night is restless
until inebriated humans
dank in sweat return home

The night is restless
till the dogs after their last
relay of barks return to the stars

till…

every cigarette
from the corner shop
returns to the ashes

a prostitute
has hidden her breasts
to return to healing

    and her man
    over sleeping bodies
    returns to his guilt

sidewalks begin to waver
thieves have found their bush,
and an old man
has had his last cough

The night is restless
until the sun resumes its duty
and laps it clean for a repeat.

At a Temple for Harijans, Mysore: Humbling Appeals

The stature of Gods
rise and sink to the tune of their class
the breadth of their shrines
& the depth of their pockets.

Here, the presiding deity doesn't
demand too much nor mind
the lowlands that dwarf the crown

Not for him diamonds to stud
his ears, but a torn rag
Not for him the sweet *payasam*,
but a slain chicken
Not for him the *dwarapalakas*
but begging palms
Not for him the solitude
a game of cards is fine
Not for him Krishna's *rasalila*,
but *kabaddi* of imps

The scope of their blessings
cures imaginary to mild infections,
grants the likelihood of a meal
or a path for a thief in the flee

that when I fold my hands,
God trembles in fear
and responds to my prayer, asks

"Please lead me out of this place
past these hounding eyes,"
I pray as he sighs in relief.

At Sahar Airport, Bombay: Hanging Mountain

We all come back
to the grace of our footing

to lick the lost sweat
that has found the spine

to brandish a rabbit
of a smile from the hat of rags,
to go misty-eyed on the fog,
to romanticize existence

only to find the stage
a mirage painted with tar

the rungs dislodged,
the mountain hangs in the air.

That the only way is up, alas.

At Sunita's Funeral, Matawan, New Jersey: Square Pegs

this is his favourite spot,
to have us by the throats

eyes on a goose chase,
minds, uninspired, rock in the dead

the sky rains blue
the sunbeams wide

parasols of grief hold up
the sky to save tears & tan

The priest chants mantras
as her petite body's ferried

across the red carpet
of faith fading under feet.

the eulogies follow fitting
square pegs on a round hole

*("She died so young because
God pined for her kindness!"
Thank God she didn't suffer!")*

**Ghenghiz Khan at Samarkand, 1258 A.D.: Shaming
the _Vedas_**

this is a flattened hierarchy
a ladder placed sideways
for the king stands not taller
but just spreads his tent wide

this is a city on the pegs
of civilization in horseshoes
cathedral's dome is the sky
Venus its cross

this is a country in flee
across the horizon flags the wind
as pollens diffuse
over jaws, never fall

here, he stands
at the feet of the Lord,
thorns pulled out from his sole
the Tigris sunk in blue

a solitary thought lazes
around the walls;
a fly in a war zone

      redeemer of a religion,
      a saviour, a gnat;

a spark of life
in murky heavens
shaming the Vedic…

      He is the kind of man.

At Velankanni Shrine, Madras: Silent Witness

a flame of one plea,
lights the next wick passing
on the baton of faith

flames weld the hands
in prayer, stake the body
on a terra firma

my prayer for a child
walks to the altar

on the side of the glass
that occludes Mary,
I avow amidst his seekers

"If it be a baby girl,
let her blossom in this fold
of prayer, let Mary be the witness!"

* *Sacred shrine of Mother Mary that is believed to grant wishes.*

At Chamundi Hills, Mysore: Healing Fest

a feast of left-overs,
a celebration of residues,
a diurnal truce
in the cradle of halcyon flames.

a time to accept,
to forgive and forget
to re-sole the feet
in the grime of irradiance,

time for the shadows;
for the *dacoits* to soak
in its healing spirit

a time for stoic minarets
to let down their guard
& prance on the infertile
rivers that rock the paddy

it is twilight
Time that is not…

At Mantralaya*, Andhra Pradesh: Green Boons

a farmer toils to bereave
the soil of its moisture
orphaned flies scrounge
as my toes slit for a home

red peppers left to dry
tan and temper in the midday sun
as a woman oils her hair
waiting for nothing to happen

a farm of green chillies
brings tears to my eyes
as kids run down the rows,
sprinkling the plants with joy

and then the branches
of a *peepal* tree
transpose into roots
for water on earth & the sky

it hasn't rained for months here
and so, when the crop is taken away
the natives contemplate the vacuum
as Gods seek the seekers' way

** A pilgrimage center for the followers of Raghavendra Swami.*

At Todar Hamlet, Coonoor, Tamil Nadu: Reverse Goal

The *Adivasi* is a point of reference,
the starting point in this changing world,
in time and space.

He is the sea-level to measure
the peaks and depths of humanity
He is the midnight to track;
the hours of progress and decline

He is higher than all cultures,
and lower than all animals
He soars above the burdens of thought
and sinks under the tugs of nature
as the world rests as a plank
under his feet, Time readies
as a bunny rabbit for a roast.

      He is the weld in the ring of creation.
      He is the undercurrent of history
      He is the river bed of blood
      He is the hub of land and sea

      He is a nation within a country,
      a faith outside a religion,
      a link that has never seen the chain.

The *Adivasi*.
He is what we all aspire
to be, by trying to be not
He is a goal in reverse.

At Annaimava's* House, Mysore: Fair Trade

Our family library
covered by ancestral dust--
shelves lined with epics
of our mundane lives, verbose poems
to commoners' mediocrities;

and these are the custodians,
two memory banks hid
in the vaults of failing organs
as our tree grows wild
in their fertile minds--

      historians who had never seen
      an arena, chroniclers
      who had not heard a clock

as each story is a keepsake
in the shrine of hearsay

where we, the couriers of progress
the spokes of a racing wheel,
would converge onto the hub
for fair trade of dates and names

Today, however, I see a sign
hung on the door, 'Library Closed,'
as the accounts of our lineage peep
through the window bars
as if inmates of an asylum.

"When is Subbamma's son getting
married?," I screamed,
"I got a new job abroad!"

** My grandmother's brother who passed away recently.*

On the City Market Sidewalk, Bangalore: Loose Change

Here, on the sidewalk,
injustice sets at dawn;
each man is a piece of cloth masking
the mosaic tiles blurred by worn-out feet
& the difference lying in the wares
that raises him to the sky

Here, in this ocean of limbs,
beggars and vendors ride
the same wave - as only
a slight curve of the fingers
& a downcast flutter of eyelids
fork the two

Here, promises are orphaned
in transit; a beggar will not ask
a vendor for alms - rather
he is his banker for loose change.

Nothing much gets sold here
except for poverty; and at the end of the day,
the Marxist dusk reduces each
to his cloth reddened by dust.

Save the beggar.

At Malleshwaram Market, Bangalore: Good Grades

nature being brought
to order at the market
like urchins in a school parade,
clumsy products of chaos taught
to put on a show;

man-made pyramids
succeeding the branches,
roses blooming from cotton threads,
gleaming in sprinkled dew
in the dawn of night suns;

displaying their best poses
like ink from a refill almost run dry,
beggars pleading for a mouth,
garlands searching for a neck;

just looking for a detour
of worthiness before the terminus,
to justify this trek; even

a bag lady to pin a rose
will do, that two can fade together,
two smiles can hang around,
long after the lips are gone.

At Hulikal Village, Karnataka: Bear Hugs

The cow's front is a mobile shrine
and its rear a coal mine to boot
for this old woman to follow
it along the street in search...

Gratefully heaping a mound
of holy dung in her hands,
she plasters a sleeve
on a roadside tree &
leaves it to the mercy of the sun,

Now late at night,
the tree looks down-
its trunk smeared with dung;
The tree trembles
in the embrace of a disaster

in a sleepy-eyed land of cows
and *sadhus* with a hand glove of bustle.

The tree waits for the dawn,
for the old woman to come back
and take off the pat of dung
and let it breathe yet again

But what about the land?

At Shivagange* Hills, Karnataka: Melting Faith

monkeys flank the steps
ready to snatch our offerings
to the Lord -

obstacles placed in the path
of salvation, evolution's past trying
to scare it away

is it God testing man's faith?
Can he carry his offerings past
these mouths, sustain
his faith past these parodies?

dark surroundings thrust belief
down the deeply entrenched eyes
of Shiva, a converted fanatic
amidst devotees that come here
wanting to believe
that rebirth takes place
behind the veils of darkness:

not chemical, spatial rather,
as out here, under the sun's
sceptical glances, and the monkeys',
it tastes like *ghee* again.

faith melts from shadow to light,
like the butter stuck to my hands.

      Or *ghee?*

A rock hill whose cave temple is famous for a legend that ghee turns into butter when rubbed on the linga.

Going on Rounds with my Uncle, Bangalore: Myocardial Infraction

If the body is the temple,
this doctor on his bike
is God come to clean the idols

as the tiny door frames
hit the roof to fit his divinity
and tall ones bow at his feet.

This terror of the micro who rules
over the entire span of gratitude
pedals faith and science in turn
from huts to mansions

as relatives stand around helplessly,
looking for signs in his expressions
on the other side of that amazing filter
that detains pain at the skin
and lets only the trickles of distress.

He lays his kit by the bedside
soothing the crystal bowl
with his palms to foretell the destiny
of cells, they collectively call a man

as life runs through clotted veins
and whistles past heaving lungs,
squeezing the last breath from ash,
the last pulse of a warped clock.

Souls climb up rungs on his thermometer
and feelings bang his stethoscope -
the infinite reduced to numbers,
as he pulls a sheet on a heart &
fumbles for a term to wrap its kindness.

At Mahabalipuram*, Tamil Nadu: Market Values

the sun chisels shapes
out of these rocks
as under the shade
a man dabs final touches
to his master's work,

      a twitch of the nose here,
      & a turn on the bosom there
      before the lava turns back into rock.

as I stand watching him create,
his eyes rocks back and forth
from the stone gripped
in his hands to the sculpture in mine;

      from the pose of an artist
swollen with the pride of his craft
      to pleading me into buying
      his wares and feeding the bellies
lining the edges of his shade

as his quote swings
between the crest of his pedigree & its ebb,
in an open market which has priced
a video game over a rock
that houses the voices of history

      shaking cultures off their toeholds
      with the whims of man, the vendor.

As I reel in a whirlpool of worth,
the sculpture slips and lands
at my feet to halve its price.

** Famous for its rock sculptures*

Travelling By Bus, Bangalore: Separation Anxieties

As the bus rattles along pot-
filled roads, my shadow stares
at me from the ground across
the window bars - two media
linked by body, I in the moving
bus and my shadow on static earth.

Dragged like a captured king
roped to a steed, wading
through ditches and under bridges,
bumping into rocks and trees,
gashing through weeds it
staggers through unseen rooms,

as each time I hear a silent
bump, a cut or a splash, I
wince in unfelt pain, uttering a
muted shriek like the kin of a
gagged victim being flogged
in a villain's movie den. At the

terminus, riders jump on its
cheeks and walk away and
I race down the steps to hug it,
to soothe its sores and dress
its wounds as it clings to my
knees quivering and beat-

two tired sods walking
home together, foot in foot.

At Elephanta Caves, Bombay: Walking Stick

A guide is always blind,
for he can only see
through eyes that throng him,

He seeks bliss in their hearts,
finds answers in their raised brows
and feels the fire in their spark.

For only they can guide him
to the thresholds of history,
to the glory trapped in his drones.

For only they can lead him
to the kings who have fled
and left these ruins as souvenirs.

For only they can wake
up bodies from their tombs,
paste noses back on bruised sculptures
With swords of Time raise a citadel
from the rubble that sink his feet.

For only they can find truth in his lies
Only they can find an epiphany
in his visceral calling, scratch
the gold gilding his guts.

A guide is always blind;
his hands on my shoulders,
mine on his.

At Indo-Pak Border, Kashmir: Split Personality

Separate a river by its banks,
dismantle bridges
that ever cross your mind…

Dike along the course,
knot lineages midstream
and drift agonies ashore

Draw lines on a map
under a cozy lamp—
a pen revels in its blood

severing a whole into parts
that you do not bear
never had to endure

It's easy; dragging bodies
over borders,
baring a girl in ruins,
fencing strangers laced with shards

With hands that once
broke bread and sliced memories
into self-contained bites

it dismembers memes
into neat limbs and digits
breaks a ritual octopus,

butchers a land to arrest
its beat… Now, do you see Jekyll?
He melds into his beat.

Visiting Grandmother, Bangalore: Deep Freeze

Grandma is obsessed
with her palms, scanning them
for future lines blurred by Time.

The hands that fed us
cannot lift a ladle, that stuffed
our school bags cannot write a word.

She is a signature rejected
at the bank, a stone being pruned
for God's foundations,
a mouth pedalling the (food) chain.

As every dawn bold-faces
her siblings on the obituaries,
she brandishes my gift from
the world trapped in her iron trunk.

"Go and buy a shirt," she tells me,
with a frostbitten rupee note.
"And get me back the change."

At Parents' Home, Bangalore: (Don't Say) Good Morning!

Every dawn,
I wake up a bit more tired,
having trekked a few more miles
through the night to close
the loop but not so quite.
I open the door to let
the sun tumble into my house
like the granny next door
who peeps in through the holes,
ears pricked for gossip.

I ogle at the sun,
if I can detect some wear
in its edges, if its rays
have been wrinkled in transit,
or by reverse osmosis
of progress on earth?

    Have the twigs forgotten
    to bloom after a long winter
    at least for a day?

Give me a sign I plead.
Please do something.
Don't just sit there.
Sigh. Fume. Cry. Don't
just anesthetically blaze me back
to sleep.

In a Hotel in Hyderabad at Night: Semantics

What's a wall to do
when tenanted on both sides,
like two rivers converging on a dike -

    a beggar propping
    his head from one side,
    my wife and I poking
    their feet from the other? With

    whom lies its allegiance?
    Who and whose assets,
    is it trying to guard? What
    is indoor and out?

Its addled door creaks
to let a burglar in and steal
from our side. And when he leaves,
the beggar locks the door from
his side and goes to sleep in peace - for,

now at least one side
is safe and secure.

    His side.

During Babri Masjid Riots, Mysore – 1: Requiem

Vultures are flying at half-
mast over the meat market,

waiting for the butcher's final stroke,

for steel to dig
into the knotted hearts of wood,
for bloody streams to be diked
by the clots of Time;

to lower the flag on the ground
and fly high again
with the dead snared in its cloth.

During Babri Masjid Riots, Mysore - 2: God's Soliloquy

My mosques and temples stare
at each other's spires in fear,
hands stretched into a sawmill
readied to be cut.

I am falling prey
to my metaphors.

    "Am I really two beings,
    a patched up doll
    whose glue is melting away?
    How can I smother my jungle
    with a grass quilt?

    Why fight with myself?
    Why hide my flaws?
    Maybe the guys know better.
    Maybe I am not one.

'Listen to the priests,
and listen to the mullahs.'

    A millennium spent in shrines
    and *kaabas* have had their toll on me.
    I've fallen into my trap.
    I've become a believer.
    Just like a land
    that believes its borders.

Jai Ram! Allah O Akbar!"

At Ellis Island*, New York: Naked Dreams

This is a percolator of cultures,
a waste basket of identities,
a plebeian sluice gate;

where you first wipe
your native soil on the doormat,
then wash the pasts off
your hands, empty memories
from your pockets and dusted
jingoistic cobwebs from your mind;

touch up holocaust scars
with cream from Ponds,
sublime the entrenched glooms
of history in an ether
of plastic smiles, make

a pledge to start anew
and keep it the same,
to never dovetail today into morrow,
nor sneak the night into dawn,

and only then,

stripped down to your bones,
a sculpture of possibilities
armed with flesh, health, wits
and a bouquet of dreams,

freed from your own self,
can you step into the land
of the free. And never look back.

* *Main port of immigration into the United States during the 1920s.*

At Srirangapatna* Fort, Near Mysore: Solar Anxieties

Leaving his crown
on the throne to rule by proxy,
the king stands atop his fort
as a farmer ambles home at a distance.

His kingdom seems
like a ring of peace
and freedom, fortress being the hole.
Who would feed a shade
to an umbrella, he muses;
who would wipe <u>its</u> tears away?

He tries to pull back the setting sun back
with his sword. True
that it would rise again tomorrow
but would it be the same sun?

He has fooled Time with history
knotting its thread with dates
and bear-hugging eternity
with the arms of a tick.

As the sun bites the dust raked
by enemy hoofs,
sirens ring for battle.
It won't be the same sun tomorrow,
he surmises,

no matter what his minions say.

** Tipu Sultan's capital*

At Kanjeevaram*, Tamil Nadu: Novelty Store

Beaded necklaces twine
around one wrist,
a begging bowl pokes out
of another towards me,

merchant
and mendicant shaking hands
at her navel
in a Darwinian alliance,

her one hand thrust forth
to peddle her wares, the other
to vend her hunger,
trying to get to my wallet
one way or the other,

and like the spokes
of an engine called India,
they alternate to inch
the train forward,

hook or (and) by
crook along the tracks
of free enterprise.

** Famous for its temples and silk sarees.*

Returning from a Trip to Mars: Litmus Test

How do I detect life
on an alien star,
get my litmus to turn violet?
How do I get souls
to thud my sixth sense? I,

who have built a cage
around my dreams!
I who grope for light switches
in the dark,

whose every invention
been an extrapolation
of knowledge, discoveries
in realms of thought. I,

who have painted my gods
white with ten palms,
and blackened my demons
with twice the fangs. The

pads from which I've launched
on many unknown wings
that gravitate me now
as the litmus in my hands
pines for the first

earthly bug I can set my eyes.

Lazing on the Culvert, Bangalore: Bargain Sale

Energized by the sun,
my shadow ticks like the hour hand
around my body clock.

This treasury of my traits,
the pallbearer of my legacy
clings to my legs mounting
a symbiotic masquerade.

This is the same shadow
which will look askance
as the kindred line up at my casket,
rustle and crackle its way
out of the grips of fire

and roam the streets, this vagrant,
luring bodies with my leftovers,
selling my traits for a dime.

    "Buy his kindness and I
    will give his pen craft for free!
    And here take all his memories,
    before you and I start afresh."

This king of parasites
will stretch a sapling, rock a cradle;
and stalk the corner to grab
the first body turning the alley
leaving my traits in the trash:

    whatever is left from its bargains.

At Dawn in the Western Ghats: Satan's Blessings

I am a twig dangling at the
treetop longing to alight the
bark and dance with weeds again,

reminiscing of days bygone
when long before there
was ever a trunk I was the plant.
When long before there
was ever a shoot I was the root.

No sir! I never aspired
to reach the top but had been
pushed up here against my own will
in this inverted Darwinian
jungle where the top
is a curse on a blessed few,
a residue of the abundant.

Whoever looks at me now? -
I, the most dispensable twig
of all dangling up in the sky
far away from my own shade,
trembling under the weight
of an eagle perched on my
feeble edge threatening
to bring me crashing down.

It is a long way from here
and I hope to make it safe.

At Alcatraz*, San Francisco Bay: Say Cheese

Bars have turned into tree stubs
for a swing as my child hops
between cell and corridor
in a blur of in and out, freedom
and shackles hand in hand,

    and we get ready to pose on
    Al Capone's bed in all smiles.

This was once a conflux of
Satans where evil reigned alone
the empire of man's mind
without the fear of an angelic siege;
where the yolk of violence
had been swept back from
the streets into a patched up shell.

But today as the sun slides
down its shadows into the cell
and scales the walls:

    fear has slipped through the cracks,
    the yolk has not left a stain
    and evil has not left even a trace,
    except for that voice that rings
    in my ears through the tour audio,
    softly and ever so calm.

There are no frigid waters to swim
through as our next ferry waits
patiently to haul us, criminals, back,
even stamping our inmate IDs
so that we don't return on the same stub.

** A former maximum-security prison on an island, now open to the public as a tourist spot.*

Hearing about Sunita's* Death, Washington D.C.: Change of Guards

The rings swim into my ears
on the ripples of laughter
as I whistle towards the phone set,
still wearing the aftermath of a smile.

The news tries to sink the waves
and erase my smile, tooth by tooth;
a vacuum aiming to suck in nature
and reverse the Pythagorean trend.

But for the next distended hour
in this layered buffer of sentiments
during a delayed change of guards,
as the sky casts glistening shadows
across my blues and a bird lowers
its feathers to tickle my heart:

life taunts me with its joys -
leeches sucking the last laugh
from my vocals for now
before they can strum another chord;

maligning every token of distress,
a smile clawing on my wails
and pupils roving the landscape
from behind my tears in search of a rose:

as Sunita patiently waited in the wings,
a garland of memories in her hands.

* A dear friend who died very young at the age of 26

At Gateway of India, Bombay: Target Practice

I see partners in crime here
and everywhere, friendships
cemented in a swampland.

I see two kids sharing a stolen bread,
mouldy crumbs sanctified by hunger.
I see prostitutes combing each other's
hair playing mothers in turn.
Sadhus are on a coffee break engaged
in a genial exchange of lies.
Vandals are passing a puff around as
rage fans itself under the shade,

all baby snakes coiled on a lap
baring smiles to evade my siren calls:

When the lap toss the snakes in fear,
the sun takes away the night's
cover and urchins spill on the
streets leaving the crumbs behind
becoming easy targets at last,

primed for my judgment.

At Central Train Station, Madras: Blurring Hops

The train is readying for departure,
but the platform clings on
like a child to its mother's saree,
field-bound.

The journey waits
patiently inside the engine,
huffing and puffing on wheels rooted
by a wall of tender hands.

Travelers and locals swap places
as a kid hops merrily
between ground and chassis,
switching allegiances
from station to journey every moment.

Trunks and bodies drowse afar,
flagging no signs
of departure - cozy homesteads

in transit. The whistle blows.
Smiles turn into tears.
Hands slide from windows
and soon turn into waves.
Human particles realign
as the kid makes up its mind at last.

And slowly but surely,
the platform slides away
with its crumbling walls,
leaving me glued to my window seat.

Visiting a Relative at Hospital, Bangalore: Solitaire

As his relatives and I form a
cordon around him
against the insurgence of *Yama*,

he feels safe like a card snuggled
in the pack lying by his bed
as my hands tightly clasp his,

    for nothing can befall him now,
    neither a virus nor a flood;
    for every card, he reckons now
    is as prime as the next
    and every lung a kernel of life.

But as the nurse beckons
us all out in single file
and our words ripple
through his ears from the corridor,

the cards shuffle themselves
right before his eyes and mine
like autumn leaves in the wind.

The shuffling stops,

popping a lone card into his hands.
He hurriedly counts the pack
to find fifty-two of them intact,

   and the one left in his hands.

Driving Along Bangalore-Mysore Road: Parboiled Rice

Along this road that has served
as a timeline to my life to date,
I see that every square inch
is green, not the wilds
of nature but fodder instead,

an industry, a busy bee,
a plate serving a billion hands,
leaving bygones behind
when it could just grow wild:

    a celebration of life, toying
    with an idea, sowing a seed;
    when a fruit was an afterthought
    and fertility was just a notion. There's

no time for all that now,
for this is the Time to feed,
a purpose to every weed,
a fruit to every seed,
and a destination to every tree.
For life is no more an idea-
It is a product multiplying itself,

when even the sky is green and
clouds rain rice directly into the gaping

    mouths. Washed and cooked.

Snake Charmer on the Sidewalk, Mysore: Balanced Diet

The snake has slithered
behind the wicker curtains
and coins have slid into their satchel.

The umbrella has been folded
up for the next rain and a lid
been shut on godliness.

The audience has scattered,
the evil in their heads
still swaying to the tunes.

It is Time for the epilogue,
to see the charms behind the charmer's life,
a free guided tour of bites,

on a body that looks
like a map of Time stung by dates,
nature's vaccines against Man,
a talisman engraved by Satan.

The snake had fed him food
and poison that rinsed each other
in a mash of nourishment
churning the myths of creation.

As my bag lies next
to his basket, we are two charmers
on a lunch break baring

our bodies, exchanging our bites.

At a Construction Site, Gulbarga*: Arch Bridge

The tree is just a sketch
on the sky canvas ashamed
of turning into a portrait.

Its shade just an illusion-
a mirage tempting the sand,
a horizon that sends
the landscape on a goose chase.

There is no water
in this desert only sweat-
an ocean full of its tang,

and this mason goaded by
by carrots of dusk and sticks
of heat and light, and by
the earth which gets aroused
by the gleam on his skin:

carries a skyscraper
of shades on his back,
one brick at a time
arching his bridge to even-
keel the burdens of ease.

* Town in the driest part of Karnataka

At Canara Bank, Mysore: Cosmic Ledger

This farmer standing behind
me in the cash counter line
hands me his passbook folded
and crumpled in his pockets,
his soiled hands smudging
the growth of money.

I see entries been made here by one
and all, in this autograph book
of literates breezing past his life
or a ledger for the cosmos to
sign in?

I see strangers shaking hands
across ledger lines and walls of creed,
keeping the account moving
and his money flowing,
as his worth bounces from one
line to the next lacing a string
of handwritings and moods.

I make my entry and walk away,
being the farmer's final tally, for now.

Walking through a Slum, Bangalore: Distress Calls

The mirror inside this hovel,
hangs high at its corner
looking down on its patrons;
as on the other corner hangs the lord
like two sentries in wonderland.

You cannot see it, for it
is too small to fit your eyes,
to fit every crack in the walls
and all realities in its trunk.

And so it does in parts,
stitching a quilt of images
in its mind all by memory
like a milkmaid keeping track
of her cans and bottles.

It shows the man's beard
only one strand at a time.
It shows the girl who jumps
in and out of its failing sight
her smile one tooth at a time.

But what about the mistress
who stands in front of it now
swaying her face left to right?
Just her sun-sized *bindi*
is enough to drown all its silver.

And what about her eyes
whose lashes cast on it a net?
And her heart. That begs for an entire lagoon.

www.ingramcontent.com/pod-product-compliance
Lightning Source LLC
LaVergne TN
LVHW041231200726
843507LV00013B/2653